GW00789399

The ABC Dinosaur

Jill Kingdon

Illustrations by Seymour Fleishman

A DINOSAUR
FOR EVERY LETTER
OF THE ALPHABET

Book

Delair Publishing Company, Inc.

ISBN: 0-8326-2622-8

Dinosaurs

The name *dinosaur* comes from two Greek words meaning "terrible" and "lizard." Actually, not all the dinosaurs were terrible and none of them were lizards, but scientists didn't know very much about them when they came up with the name.

Dinosaurs roamed the earth millions of years ago—before any people were here. There are no dinosaurs alive today, so we say they are *extinct*. To find out what the dinosaurs looked like and how they lived, we must study the fossils of their bones, eggs and footprints. We also look at the fossils of plants and insects that lived in the Age of

Dinosaurs to learn more about life at that time.

Dinosaurs were all reptiles, but they came in a variety of shapes, sizes and types. Some were no larger than chickens, and some longer than three school buses. Some were calm and gentle and ate plants; others were fast and ferocious and ate other dinosaurs! Heavy armor covered one group and strange crests topped another.

The dinosaurs ruled the earth for about 120 million years. Then rather suddenly, they disappeared. We don't know why they all died; that is one of the mysteries still surrounding them.

There are many, many other mysteries, as well. A lot of what we "know" about these magnificent creatures is guesswork. We have found few complete skeletons of the different dinosaurs. For example, as popular as Brontosaurus is, we have never found a skeleton of him with his head attached. So all of our models and pictures of him, known by school children worldwide, are just opinions of what he looked like.

The study of dinosaurs is a new study—only about 150 years old! We have much to learn, and much of what we think we know will probably be proven wrong with new discoveries. We are pioneers in this field, and there is a vast frontier of information yet to be discovered.

Ankylosaurus
(ANG kul o sawr us)

Ankylosaurus looked like a walking army tank as he roved about looking for soft juicy plants to eat. Oval plates protected his head, body and tail; and sharp spikes protected his legs and belly. If another dinosaur tried to hurt him, he dropped to the ground and swung his clubbed tail at his attacker. The only way an enemy could hurt him was to roll him over on his back and attack his soft belly.

Brachiosaurus
(brak ee o SAWR us)

Before the discovery of a new dinosaur being called "Supersaurus," Brachiosaurus was thought to be the largest dinosaur of them all. He was as heavy as twenty elephants and as tall as a four-story building. Scientists have changed their minds about some other ideas they had about Brachiosaurus, as well. No longer is it believed that he spent most of his time in the water, ate only soft plants, or had two brains. Now we think that his lungs probably would have collapsed underwater, that he ate bark and twigs, and that he had only one real brain. We still don't know why he had his nostrils on top of his head.

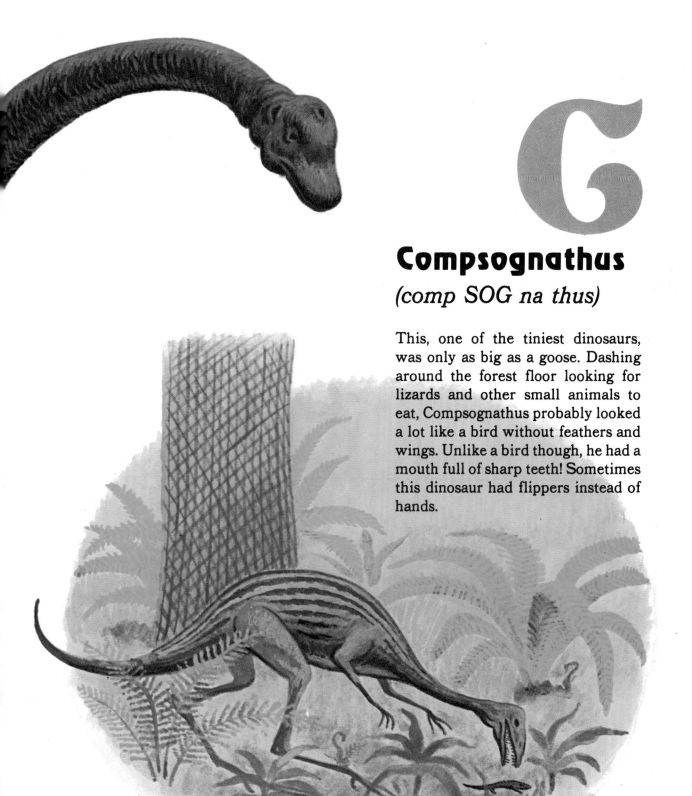

G

Compsognathus
(comp SOG na thus)

This, one of the tiniest dinosaurs, was only as big as a goose. Dashing around the forest floor looking for lizards and other small animals to eat, Compsognathus probably looked a lot like a bird without feathers and wings. Unlike a bird though, he had a mouth full of sharp teeth! Sometimes this dinosaur had flippers instead of hands.

Diplodocus
(di PLOD o cus)

Diplodocus was one of the longest dinosaurs—as long as three school buses. He had a very long tail and a very long neck with a tiny head. His brain was as tiny as a kitten's. Even though Diplodocus was huge, he was gentle and ate only plants. Diplodocus, like Brachiosaurus, breathed through nostrils on the top of his head.

Edmontosaurus
(ed MONT o sawr us)

Edmontosaurus was the largest of the duck-billed dinosaurs. Besides having a head like a duck, he probably swam like one, too. We think he had webbed hands and feet that helped him swim quickly away when a meat-eater tried to catch him. Different from a duck, though, Edmontosaurus had teeth—over 2,000 of them! He used them to grind up the plants he ate. When one tooth got worn out, another grew in its place.

Fabrosaurus
(fa bra SAWR us)

This three-foot tall dinosaur stayed in dry, hilly places rather than risk a meeting with a ferocious meat-eater in the swamps. Fabrosaurus spent his days looking for plants to eat. His horny beak helped him break off stems and leaves, and his flat teeth were good at grinding them up. His hind legs were much longer and stronger than his front legs or "arms." This tells us that he was able to stand on his hind legs, and that he was probably a fast runner.

G

Gorgosaurus
(gor go SAWR us)

Gorgosaurus was a dangerous enemy to other dinosaurs. He was able to run quickly, and his huge jaws were filled with teeth like knives. His sharp claws could rip through the tough skin of other dinosaurs. Gorgosaurus looked and acted a lot like the larger king of the meat-eaters, Tyrannosaurus Rex. No wonder Gorgosaurus means "terrible reptile."

Hypsilophodon
(hip si LOFF o don)

Hypsilophodon has been called the "kangaroo of the dinosaurs" because he used his tail for balance and could jump and run so well. His speed was probably the only thing that saved him from being eaten by the meat-eaters. He had practically no teeth or armor. Herds of hysilophodon wandered along coastlines looking for fruit and soft vegetables to eat.

14

Iguanodon
(ig WAN o don)

The very first dinosaur bone to be discovered by man belonged to Iguanodon. As tall as a house, Iguanodon walked on his powerful hind lengs. On his hands, he had enormous claws where his thumbs should have been. He used his claws to stab his enemy during fights. Iguanodon fought only to protect himself, though, since he was a plant-eater. We know that these dinosaurs travelled in herds because twenty skeletons were found together in a coal mine in Belgium.

Jaxartosaurus

(jacks ART o sawr us)

Jaxartosaurus was a duck-bill dinosaur. He walked on all fours most of the time, standing on his hind legs only to run or reach into a tree for some pine needles or twigs to eat. His tail was long and flat, almost like the rudder on a boat. He used it to drive himself through the water when he swam. Like all the duck-bill dinosaurs, he probably had webbed feet and hands. Although he was a good swimmer, Jaxartosaurus lived on the land.

K

Kentrosaurus
(Kent ro SAWR us)

The name Kentrosaurus means
"prickly lizard," and it is easy to see
why he was named that. A double
row of bony plates protected his
head and neck, and several pairs of
long, sharp spikes protected his body
and tail. During a fight, Kentrosaurus would turn his back to his
enemy and lash out with his barbed
tail. Herds of these dinosaurs lived in
swampy areas and ate plants.

Lambeosaurus

(lam be o SAWR us)

Lambeosaurus was a duck-bill dinosaur who had a strange V-shaped crest on top of his head. No one knows exactly why he had the crest. Some people think it gave him a better sense of smell. Some think it gave him a louder "voice." Others believe the different shaped crests helped duck-bill dinosaurs tell each other apart. Why do *you* think Lambeosaurus had the crest?

Megalosaurus

(meg a lo SAWR us)

Megalosaurus is known for being one of the most successful animals that ever lived. His body was perfectly made for the life he led. His back legs were long and powerful to help him run quickly after the dinosaurs he ate. His jaws had powerful muscles and rows of very large teeth with saw-tooth edges. The Megalosaurus family survived for over 90 million years. That's a long time when you think that Man has been on earth for only 2 million years!

Nodosaurus

(node o SAWR us)

Nodosaurus was a heavily armored dinosaur like Ankylosaurus. His back was completely covered with a shell of bony plates. He looked something like a huge turtle. His tail also had a hard covering. Even his head had a sort of thick "roof" covering it. Nodosaurus grew to be longer than most cars and was a plant-eater.

Ornitholestes
(orn i tho LESS teez)

Ornitholestes was a little bit taller than a man but weighed much less. His name means "bird robber" because the scientist who named him thought his long, clawed fingers were used to catch birds. Ornitholestes ate the animals that were too small and fast for the larger meat-eaters.

P Protoceratops
(prot o SER a tops)

Protoceratops is a very important dinosaur. Discovered along with many Protoceratops skeletons were Protoceratops eggs. Because of this finding we learned that dinosaurs laid eggs. Before that we didn't know how dinosaur babies were born. From the Protoceratops fossils, scientists could tell that the mother probably laid her eggs, about twenty at a time, in a shallow hole. She then covered them with sand and left them to hatch in the sun. The mother stayed close by, though, and protected her eggs.

Quetsalcoatlus
(kwet sole CO at lus)

and

Rhamphorhyncus
(ram fo RINK us)

Quetsalcoatlus and Rhamphorhyncus were not true dinosaurs. They were flying reptiles who lived during the Age of Dinosaurs. Quetsalcoatlus is the largest flying creature that has ever lived. His wingspan was 50 feet. He probably floated on air currents, setting down to feed on dead animals. Rhamphorhyncus lived before Quetsalcoatlus and led a different kind of life. Rhamphorhyncus was a fisherman, swooping down and scooping up fish much like our pelicans do. He was similar to the pelican in size, too. Unlike a pelican, though, this flying reptile had teeth and a long tail with a rudder to help him steer.

Stegosaurus

(steg o SAWR us)

Stegosaurus had an unusual armor. He had two rows of bony triangles going down his backbone, and each triangle was as tall as a three-year-old child! Any meat-eater who bit Stegosaurus' back took the chance of breaking his teeth or being hit by the powerful tail with its four sharp spikes. Although this plant-eater was very long and heavier than a car, his head was quite small and contained a brain the size of a walnut.

Tyrannosaurus Rex

(tie ran o SAWR us

wrecks)

Tyrannosaurus Rex, "King of the Tyrant Reptiles," was the most powerful animal ever to walk this planet. If Tyrannosaurus were alive today, he'd be able to see in an upstairs window with his feet still on the ground, and he'd outweigh the largest elephant. He was so big that his eye socket was the size of a human head and his toe claws were the size of carving knives! His mouth could open wide enough to hold a large dog. Tyrannosaurus Rex was the biggest and most feared of all the meat-eaters.

Uintasaurus

(yoo IN ta sawr us)

Uintasaurus was a very long, heavy plant-eater. He had a small head and a long, pointy tail. He was in the same family as Brachiosaurus and Diplodocus and looked a lot like them. Another name for Uintasaurus is Camarasaurus (ca MAR a sawr us).

Velociraptor

(vel oss a RAP ter)

Velociraptor's name means "swift robber." He was named that because it is believed he may have robbed baby Protoceratops from their nests and eaten them. Velociraptor had arms and hands that he used to catch and hold his dinner. He was a fast runner with big eyes and a large brain.

Walgettosuchus
(wol ge toe SUKE us)

All we know about Walgettosuchus is that he was a meat-eater, he could run fast on hind legs and he had long fingers. Paleontologists, or people who study fossils, have found only a few parts of Walgettosuchus' skeleton so far. Until more parts are found, the mystery of this dinosaur remains unsolved.

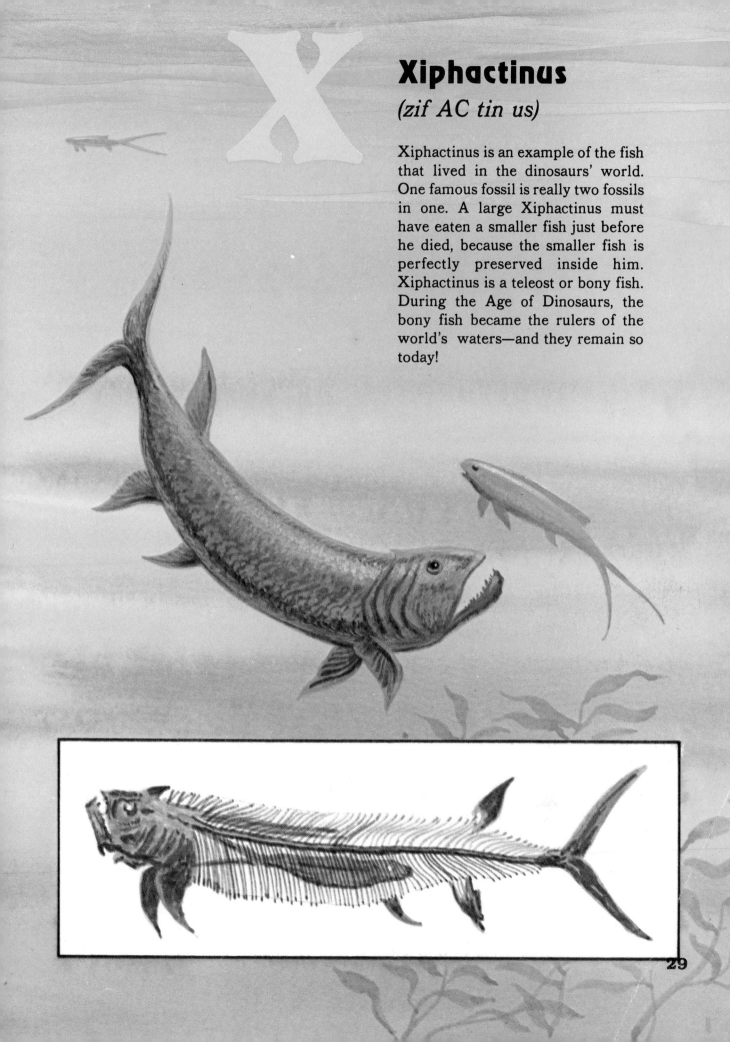

Xiphactinus
(zif AC tin us)

Xiphactinus is an example of the fish that lived in the dinosaurs' world. One famous fossil is really two fossils in one. A large Xiphactinus must have eaten a smaller fish just before he died, because the smaller fish is perfectly preserved inside him. Xiphactinus is a teleost or bony fish. During the Age of Dinosaurs, the bony fish became the rulers of the world's waters—and they remain so today!

Yaleosaurus

(yale o SAWR us)

This is the skeleton of Yaleosaurus. He lived at the beginning of the Age of Dinosaurs. He probably ate both plants and animals. He wasn't too tall—only a little taller than a man—and he was a clumsy runner. Another name for Yaleosaurus is Anchisaurus.

Z

Zanclodon
(ZANK lo don)

We don't know very much about Zanclodon. About all we know for certain is that he was a theropod. Theropods were mostly meat-eating dinosaurs who walked on strong hind legs and had grasping hands. Perhaps some day soon someone will find more Zanclodon fossils for us to learn from.